Short Nature Walks
on Cape Cod
and the Vineyard

Short Nature Walks on Cape Cod and the Vineyard

Hugh *and* Heather Sadlier

An East Woods Book

The
Globe
Pequot
Press

CHESTER, CONNECTICUT

ISBN 0-87106-674-2

Manufactured in the United States of America
Third Edition / First Printing

Introduction

Cape Cod's hiking trails lead to an endless variety of pleasures and discoveries. A sample of what awaits you includes sunsets topping shifting sand dunes, shaded walks along needle-covered paths coupled with eye-stretching vistas across sand and marsh, blossoming shad bush, beach plums, and *Rosa rugosa,* peaceful wanderings along deserted, snow-flecked trails, and—of course—wildlife: from cottontail rabbits with twitching noses and bobbing tails to the graceful soaring of majestic ospreys; from sideways scamperings of fiddler crabs to raucous callings of herring gulls.

The Twenty-eight Walks

Twenty-one of the walks in this book are on Cape Cod; seven are on Martha's Vineyard. They explore woods, marshes, swamps, seashores, dunes, kettle holes, drumlins, ponds, streams, and wildlife sanctuaries. They take you to an island and a braille trail. All follow established trails that are either well marked or easily recognized.

Most of the walks provide opportunities to observe and appreciate nature at a leisurely pace. A few will challenge your muscles and bring sweat to your brow.

New Areas

The mid-1980s saw a substantial increase in the number of properties acquired by towns and foundations for conservation purposes. The trails for many of these areas were in the planning and development stages while we were preparing this book's third edition. For information on new trails not described in this edition, please contact the following offices and groups:

Conservation Commissions/Natural Resource Departments/ Town Halls

Barnstable Natural Resources Department 617-775-1120
1189 Phinney's Lane
Barnstable, MA 02630

Bourne Conservation Commission   617-759-8145
165 State Road
Bourne, MA 02532

Brewster Conservation Office   617-896-3701
Town Hall
Brewster, MA 02631

Chatham Conservation Foundation   617-945-4084
104 Crowell Road
Chatham, MA 02633

Chatham Town Hall   617-945-2100
549 Main Street
Chatham, MA 02633

Eastham Conservation Office   617-255-0333
County Road
Eastham, MA 02642

Falmouth Natural Resources Department   617-548-7355
750 Main Street
Falmouth, MA 02540

Harwich Conservation Commission   617-432-2143
Town Hall
Harwich, MA 02645

Mashpee Conservation Office   617-477-1866
Great Neck Road
Mashpee, MA 02649

Sandwich Conservation Commission   617-888-4200
Town Hall Annex
Sandwich, MA 02563

Truro Conservation Commission   617-349-2748
Town Hall

Town Hall Road
Truro, MA 02666

Wellfleet Conservation Commission   617-349-3708
Town Hall
Wellfleet, MA 02667

Yarmouth Conservation Office   617-394-3508
Town Hall
Yarmouth, MA 02675

Getting Ready

Use your common sense to select clothing for these excursions.
Footwear demands the most attention. You'll want sturdy-but-com-
fortable, flat-soled shoes (a solid pair of sneakers would be suffic-
ient for most of the walks). On longer treks, particularly the ones
through soft sand, you should consider over-the-ankle shoes or boots
to give extra support and keep sand out of your socks.

None of the walks call for specialized clothing beyond that already
mentioned. We suggest wearing loose-fitting, comfortable clothes
geared to the season and weather you're hiking in.

For the longer walks such as Sandy Neck and Great Island, you'll
want to put more thought into preparations. You'd be wise to start
early in the day to avoid the summer sun. Your trip will be much
more enjoyable if you also carry a supply of water with you.

Caution . . .

There are only four real "dangers" to Cape and Vineyard walkers.
Three—and hopefully all four—can be avoided by taking some pre-
cautions.

Too much sun can burn you and possibly cause sunstroke. Schedule the few longer walks in this book for early morning to avoid the
midday sun's intense heat. Take hats and protective lotion with you
even on some of the shorter hikes that briefly expose you to the sun.

Poison ivy grows abundantly on dunes and in wooded areas along
many of these walks. It can be an erect shrub, a trailing vine, or a

climber. Its three leaves may be shiny or dull, green or red, coarsely toothed or smooth-edged. Learn to recognize the plant and avoid it and anything that comes in contact with it.

A walk on any of these trails may aquaint you (and/or your dog) with two other Cape and Vineyard residents: the deer tick (*Ixodes dammini*), which may transmit Lyme disease, and the common American dog tick (*Dermacentor variabilis*), which may carry other diseases, including the less common Rocky Mountain Spotted Fever.

Lyme disease, named for the town in Connecticut where it was first recognized in 1975, is caused by corkscrew-shaped bacteria called spirochetes, which are transmitted to people by the bite of the pinhead-sized deer tick. All stages of the deer tick (larva, nymph, and adult) bite humans. Some bitten by a tick carrying Lyme disease may or may not develop a characteristic "bull's-eye" rash. Flulike symptoms, including chills, fever, fatigue, headache, nausea, muscle and joint pain, and swollen glands, are common within a week to a month. Later symptoms, which may occur up to a year after the tick bite, include arthritis, meningitis, and neurological and cardiac problems. Timely treatment with antibiotics can cure the disease or lessen the severity of later complications. Therefore, if you are bitten by a tick or if you develop any of these symptoms, it is very important to see a doctor and mention the possibility of Lyme disease. Both Lyme disease and Rocky Mountain Spotted Fever are treated with antibiotics. The following preventive measures can reduce your chances of being bitten by a tick:

1. Tuck your pant legs into your socks. Tuck your shirt into your pants. This will help keep the ticks on the outside of your clothes where they can be readily seen and removed.

2. Wear light-colored clothing. The dark-colored ticks are more visible on this light background.

3. While walking, check your clothes often for ticks.

4. Apply insect repellents (according to label instructions) to shoes, socks, cuffs, and pant legs.

5. When you return from a walk, check—or have someone else check—your head and body thoroughly for ticks.

If you find a tick embedded in your skin, remove it by gently pulling it off with tweezers, being careful not to squeeze or crush it. Wash your hands afterward. Save the tick to show the doctor.

The annoying attack of other kinds of insects, such as mosquitoes or biting flies, can take the fun out of any walk, especially those passing through or near woods and swampy areas. Keep a good repellent handy just in case.

Rules and Regulations

Rules and regulations have been developed to help us preserve natural areas and the wildlife living there. Many areas have posted signs and printed literature detailing "dos and don'ts" that should be adhered to. Please remember the following while walking:

Stay on marked trails.
Camp, cook, hunt, and fish only where permitted.
Don't cut trees, branches, or flowers.
Keep dogs on a leash.
Carry out empty what you carried in full.
Take only pictures.

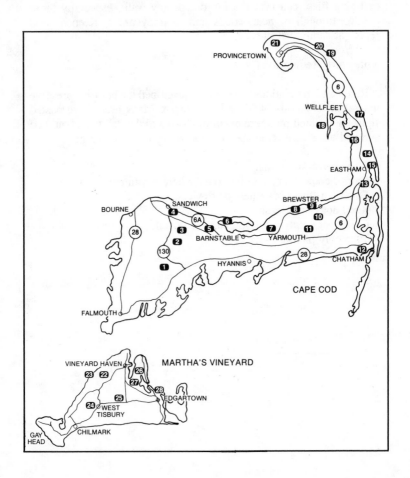

PROVINCETOWN

WELLFLEET

EASTHAM

BREWSTER

SANDWICH

BOURNE

BARNSTABLE

YARMOUTH

HYANNIS

CHATHAM

CAPE COD

FALMOUTH

MARTHA'S VINEYARD

VINEYARD HAVEN

EDGARTOWN

WEST TISBURY

GAY HEAD

CHILMARK

Contents

Cape Cod

1. Ashumet Holly Reservation

The late Wilfred Wheeler was foremost among many dedicated individuals who created splendid horticultural collections at the reservation. He gathered holly trees from all over the Cape, the islands, and other New England locations. Mr. Wheeler developed winter-hardy strains from some of the older trees still growing in the reservation.

Mr. and Mrs. Josiah K. Lilly III purchased Wilfred Wheeler's property after his death in 1961 and donated the unique, 45-acre collection to the Massachusetts Audubon Society. Varieties of Oriental and European hollies and other native plants also grow there.

Pass beside the row of pines left of the barn to a tiny clearing. Walk left down the hill toward Grassy Pond.

Continuing parallel to, but above the water, the path reaches a trail junction where a blue marker points left. Instead, go right. Cross over the ramp and meander along the pond's edge. Pink lady's slipper grows abundantly here. Catbirds enjoy the habitat provided by thick trees and shrubs near the water. Mewing calls punctuate their squeaky songs.

Continue along the shore and take the second trail leading left. Just before this turn you'll see the start of the numbered stations identified in the Holly Trail pamphlet.

Walk through an evergreen forest past the start of the Crater Loop Trail (on the right). Bear left at the fork ahead, continuing to follow the consecutively numbered stations. Turn left at the T intersection. Walk as far as station 28 on the left, then retrace your steps to the T junction, and continue past a bench on your left. Swing sharply right at station 30. Here you'll see franklinia. John Bartram discovered the last wild franklinia along Georgia's Altamaha River in 1790. This unusual shrub flowers in the fall.

Go left at a four-trail intersection ahead and bear right at the next fork. The trees and plants in the nursery area to the left of station 38 include magnolias, heaths, and dogwoods.

Branch right at the intersection near station 40 onto the English Holly Trail. Keep left at the next intersection and left again onto an old road. Follow it back to the start of the English Holly Trail.

Go sharply right (past station 41) and turn left, guided by a trail

Distance (around reservation): 1.25 miles

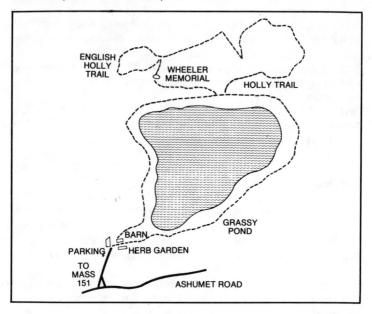

On Route 151, drive east 4 miles from Mass-28 in North Falmouth or west 3 miles from the Mashpee traffic circle. The Ashumet Holly Reservation lies on the north side of the road in East Falmouth. Follow Massachusetts Audubon Society signs to the reservation and the small parking area across from the large, weathered barn.

An admission charge of $3.00 for adults and $2.00 for children and seniors is requested for each car. In the barn, you'll find a small information center and two self-guiding trail booklets that cost $1.00 each.

sign, into a clearing. A variety of holly trees ring the open area. The Wheeler Memorial marker sits to the left. Pause and relax here on one of the reservation's many benches.

Bear right at the memorial stone and follow this route, which parallels the Pond Trail (below to the right). These two paths join a short distance ahead. Step down to the Pond Trail and go left for the return trip around Grassy Pond.

You're apt to see glimpses of pond life along this route. During dry weather the semiaquatic ribbon snake frequents the muddy shore. You'll see black bullheads, commonly called catfish, wriggling in the shallows in search of food among underwater plant stems. Belted kingfishers chatter from their perches in overhanging pine branches.

You may also see a painted turtle along the water's edge. Its dark upper shell contrasts sharply with vivid yellow head and neck markings. Usually found in shallow, weedy waters, it feeds mostly on plants. But sharp, bony jaws enable it to eat small animals—either dead or alive.

After circling the pond, you'll reach the trail intersection where a sign directs you left to the barn. Walk through the extensive herb garden back to the parking area.

2. Lowell Holly Reservation

An intriguing, well-kept network of trails laces Lowell Holly Reservation's varied woodlands. Actually a 130-acre peninsula, the reservation divides Wakeby Pond and Mashpee Pond—two of the largest freshwater ponds on Cape Cod. In addition to hiking, this area encourages nature study, fishing, swimming, and picnicking.

Abbott Lawrence Lowell, president of Harvard University from 1909 to 1933, gave the property to the Trustees of Reservations in 1943. The reservation remains open to the public daily from 10:00 A.M. to sunset between May 30 and October 12. A parking charge or boat landing fee of $2.50 is collected on holidays and weekends. An annual boat permit is available from the warden, who is on duty on summer weekends and holidays.

The trail leads left through a clearing with picnic tables and bears right toward Wakeby Pond after passing two short spurs on the right. From the pond's edge, it turns left and reaches an iron bar gate. Continue straight at the fork just ahead, following the white, circular blazes.

Note the contrasting trees along this shady route: the smooth-barked beeches, medium-smooth hollies (with sharp-tipped leaves), and the rougher pitch pines. The way bends sharply left and reaches a fork just before the pond's shore. Go right. Listen for the calls of rufous-sided towhees (*drink-your-tea*), gray catbirds (mewing calls), and common flickers (*flick or flicker*). Flickers are the only woodpeckers that commonly feed on the ground. They eat ants, primarily, plus a variety of other insects and wild fruit. These brownish birds sport bright yellow under tail and wing surfaces, red neck napes, and (in the male) a black moustache. Watch for their undulating flight and flashing white rumps.

Reaching another fork, follow the triangular white blazes left (circular white blazes lead right) onto the Wheeler Trail. Note the shade-and-moisture-loving Solomon's seal to either side of the trail here. Tubular, greenish-white flowers hang pendulously from between the leaves. Scars on its rootstock, likened to the seal of Solomon, give the plant its name. Each winter its arching, leafy stem dies, leaving a scar on the plant's root; thus, you can easily determine how old each plant is by counting the marks on the root.

7

Distance (round trip): 2 miles

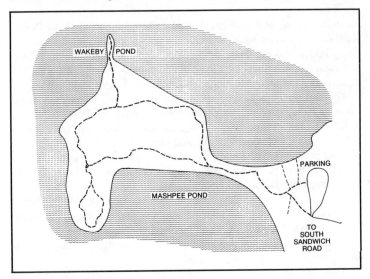

Take the Route 130 exit from U.S. 6 in Sandwich and follow it south 7.3 miles to South Sandwich Road. Turn left and drive .7 miles to the small green and white sign for the Lowell Holly Reservation. A narrow dirt road leads to the parking area.

After winding through stands of white pines, the path reaches another fork. Follow the arrows left for a loop walk over slightly elevated land. Occasional overlooks to Mashpee Pond appear through openings in the trees. Arriving back at the loop intersection, retrace your steps to the start of the Wheeler Trail and go left (following the white circles again).

Watch for multi-zoned polystictus growing on dead and downed trees through here. These pore fungi have leathery fans marked by varied, dull-colored bands. Due to their distinctive markings and shape, they have been nicknamed "turkey tails."

Reaching yet another fork, bear left onto the trail blazed with white squares. This path brings you out onto a narrow spit of land. Bushes pinch in from both sides before the way climbs a short grade and reaches a clearing. Although views are somewhat restricted by growing trees, you might hear the quacks of waterfowl on nearby waters.

Return to the most recent fork and swing sharply left, following white circles again. Passing large clusters of rhododendron and mountain laurel, the path nears the water once more. It is often difficult to tell these shrubs apart. Both have woody stems, shiny, leathery leaves (laurel's 2 to 5 inches long; rhododendron's 3 to 8 inches) and five-petaled flowers. The mountain laurel's cup-shaped flower is medium-sized. The large rhododendron flower is open and starlike.

The trail dips into damp, shady areas overflowing with ferns before returning you to the intersection near the bar gate. Go left, back to the parking area.

If conditions are right, how about that picnic and swim?

3. Wakeby Holly Sanctuary and Recreation Area

Native holly trees 50 feet high and 100 to 150 years old, fine stands of smooth-barked beeches, and towering pines, which once attracted nesting eagles, fill the Wakeby Holly Sanctuary and Recreation Area. The eagles are gone now, but other wildlife thrive in the natural cover throughout the sanctuary. A quiet stroll along the varied network of trails may bring you face to face with some of these wild creatures. Come prepared, too, for swimming, boating, and fishing (Wakeby Pond boasts some of the finest Cape Cod freshwater fishing).

The Sandwich Conservation Commission acquired this 145-acre woodland and began developing it into a natural recreational area in the summer of 1975 (additional trails will be added in the future). A modest entrance fee will be charged to non-Sandwich residents.

Walk over the rise beyond the parking area and bear right off the road onto the trail. The needle-covered path winds through pines and oaks. Hollies abound through here. Mushrooms dot the trail at ankle height.

Go either way at the fork ahead. The left fork leads down through thick woods, the right one approaches Wakeby Pond and swings left along the water's edge to join with the first a short distance ahead.

Take the next side trail on the left. It leads to a smaller clearing where you can sit and relax, refreshed by the breezes from Wakeby Pond.

Walk right from the clearing down to the Nature Center. Formerly a screen house, where harvested cranberries were dumped, separated, tested for soundness, and barreled, the completely rebuilt structure now houses many interesting nature exhibits.

Retrace your steps to the clearing and to the main trail next to the water. Swing left, through continuing beeches, to an open area near an old sluiceway (the wide trail entering from the left will be your return route to your car).

Go straight along the dike at the water's edge, past the old cranberry bog. The path soon splits above a depression. Go right for a walk through a heavily forested area. Once again, beeches predominate. The small, triangular beech nuts provide nourishment for such area residents as quail, raccoons, deer, rabbits, and squirrels.

Distance (round trip): 2.1 miles

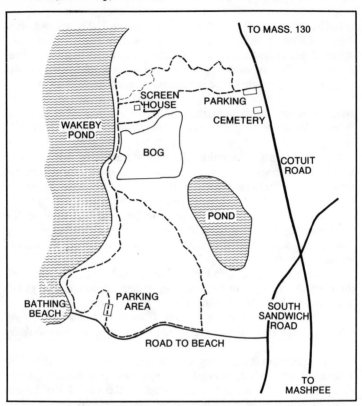

Take the Mass 130 exit off U.S. 6 in Sandwich and drive south 1.6 miles. Turn left onto Cotuit Road and follow it 4.8 miles to the dirt road on the right (just beyond a large cranberry bog) leading to the parking area.

The trail reaches a clearing near a tiny cove. Turn left from the clearing onto a wider path and follow its looping route to a parking area. Go straight through the parking lot to the entrance road and turn left. Follow it .35 miles to the trail leading left.

This shady route passes down through oaks, beeches, and hollies to junction with a wider trail. Go left to a small clearing and continue on the trail leading straight ahead. This path meanders past a secluded 5-acre pond that was once used as a nursery for otters. Today it provides an ideal habitat for a variety of waterfowl.

The soft, spongy path passes through towering maples before reaching the fork above the depression. Bear right, cross the dike, and follow the wide path $1/4$ mile back to the parking area.

THE OLD
BRIAR PATCH

THORNTON W BURGESS
CHILDREN'S AUTHOR · NATURALIST

4. The Old Briar Patch

"If I should walk in Gully Lane
Think you that I would find
The boyhood lost so long ago
The youth I left behind?
Are still the days so carefree there?
So filled with simple joy?
So heedless of the march of time
As when I was a boy.
Would clutching hands of bramble bush
Still reach to hold me fast
Or would thou treat me as a ghost—
A vision from the past?
Would summer berries taste as sweet?
The wild grapes spice the air
With quite the winey fragrance that
In memory haunts me there?

Ah me! So many years have fled
And mingled joy with pain
I fear to seek the boy who once
Did walk in Gully Lane."

Thornton W. Burgess reflects upon both his boyhood days in the Gully Lane area and the wide-eyed enthusiasm that all too often disappears as we "mature" in today's complex society. Noted author of seventy children's books and 15,000 bedtime stories, Burgess was born in Sandwich in 1874. His love of nature and the foundation for his nature stories originated in the woodland now called the Old Briar Patch. The people of Sandwich sponsored this attractive 57-acre area in 1974 in honor of Mr. Burgess.

You're liable to see many of the fabled Burgess characters somewhere within the Old Briar Patch. Watch and listen for Sammy Jay, Peter and Mrs. Rabbit, Reddy Fox, Old Mr. Toad, Jimmy Skunk, Johnny Chuck, Hooty Owl, Bobby Coon, and maybe even Paddy Beaver. Take time to look, listen, smell—and recapture those spontaneous awakenings of earlier days.

Distance (round trip): 2 miles

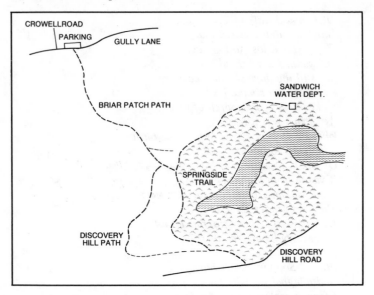

Turn south onto Chipman Road from Mass 6A, either 1.1 miles east of the Sandwich Police Department or 2.3 miles west of the East Sandwich Post Office. At the road's end, turn left onto Crowell Road. Follow it to the end and turn left onto Gully Lane. Park beside the split rail fence 150 feet ahead.

Bullbriers proliferate near the trail's starting point, providing ideal living areas for Peter and Mrs. Rabbit. The large, leathery leaves are rounded or heart-shaped. Numerous strong prickles along the stems offer protected hiding places for cottontail rabbits.

Pine needles blanket the wood chip path as it weaves pleasantly through shady woods. Rustic benches invite you to pause and enjoy the peaceful surroundings.

The way passes through two old stone walls. One wonders how this land used to look before early settlers spent backbreaking hours clearing trees and stones to prepare fields for farming.

After passing through a grove of deeply furrowed black locust trees, the path dips down to a swampy area and intersects the Springside Trail. Turn right and meander through shady beeches to the signed trail junction ahead. Turn sharply right and climb the moderate grade up Discovery Hill. Watch for the nervous movements of chipmunks in the stone wall to your left. Listen for the *bob white* call of quail from the field beyond.

Flattening out, the trail tops Discovery Hill and leads into a secluded clearing ringed by gigantic eastern white pines. More benches encourage you to enjoy this private spot and perhaps reflect upon the message in Thornton Burgess's poem.

Twisting and turning, the trail returns you to the intersection near the swampy area. Swing down to the Springside Trail and go left for a cooling walk as far as the Sandwich Water Department building. Thick grapevines crowd this section of trail.

Return to the swamp intersection and go right onto the Briar Patch Path. Retrace your original route to your starting point.

5. Talbot's Point Salt Marsh Wildlife Reservation

Talbot's Point protrudes into the Great Marsh surrounding Scornton Creek. Numerous bowers along the peninsula's edge encourage pauses for marsh watching. Green waves of wind-tossed grasses, peacefulness pierced only by wildlife activity, and rich, earthy smells are some of the natural tranquilizers to be discovered along the way.

Take the left trail from the clearing (through pitch pines) and bear right at a fork. Pass into a huge stand of red pines. There's a noticeable stillness to this area. Keeping the red pines on your left, cut right to the main trail. Then swing left.

Mourning doves may startle you with whistling wings as they take flight at your approach. Note their slim bodies, pointed wings, and tapered tails. When walking, their heads bob with each step.

The trail is actually an old road. Unpainted bird houses dot occasional trees and blend well with the surroundings.

Take the second side trail to the left (a trail opposite goes right). It leads quickly to a marsh overlook where you can see the state game farm. Ten thousand quail are raised there annually.

There are frequent views of the marsh as the trail swings right, still close to the marsh's edge. Rabbits find ideal habitats in the thick, trailside briers.

At a clearing a short trail leads right to the main trail. But go left here, continuing along the marsh's edge. Enjoy a rest and marsh view at the rough-hewn bench in the clearing ahead.

Walk through thicker pine woods on a needled trail. Make sure you stay on the path—this area is loaded with poison ivy.

Continue through bare-branched pines to another clearing with a spur leading left and a short path leading right to the main trail and a small cabin. Stay straight here, circling around the point's perimeter. The trail curves back toward the cabin. Go left at the fork ahead and left again at a second fork.

This damper area teems with ferns. After curling along the marsh's border, the path eventually enters pine woods. In late spring you may surprise a ruffed grouse. If accompanied by chicks, the hen will go into her broken wing act to entice you away from the young.

Distance (round trip): 1.5 miles

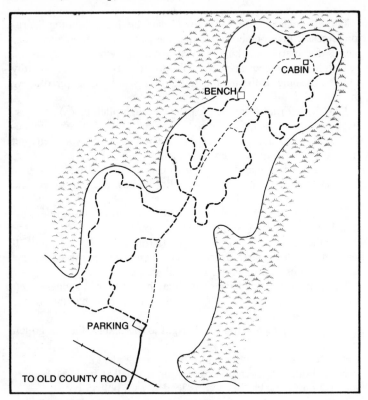

Turn south onto Old County Road opposite the East Sandwich Post Office on Mass 6A. After 1.4 miles turn left onto a wide, sandy road. Cross the railroad tracks and park in the small cleared area. Dr. and Mrs. Fritz B. Talbot gave this land to the Sandwich Conservation Commission in 1963. Camping and open fires are not permitted here.

When she has successfully diverted the danger, she'll thunder into the air and return to her chicks.

Eventually, this path rejoins the main trail directly opposite the original side trail you took. Go left onto the main trail and then right onto the next side trail.

This path winds beside the red pine woods. Look through openings on the right across cranberry bogs to the game farm's pheasant enclosures. Pass through a beech forest, climb a slight rise, and walk ahead to the parking area.

6. Sandy Neck

However you look at them, the sand dunes at Sandy Neck are impressive. They are 6.2 miles long, from 200 yards to ½ mile wide, and over 4,000 years old. Ranging from flats to mini-mountains, the dunes look like angry waves on a storm-tossed sea.

Sheltered in Sandy Neck's southerly lee, the 3,000-acre Great Marshes began to form some 3,500 years ago. Today the marshes support an extensive chain of marine life and provide protection and food for both sea and land birds.

The vastness of these traditional Cape Cod natural features will awe you as you walk through Sandy Neck. Come prepared for hiking, swimming, sunbathing, beachcombing, bird watching, and fishing.

This hike's route passes through soft sand, the sun can become unbearably hot, and there is little shelter along the way. Only persons in excellent physical condition should attempt this trek. Also, make sure you have water, suntan lotion, sturdy footwear (preferably to ankle tops), and a good knowledge of your route. Hike in the early morning to avoid the midday sun (and increase your chances of seeing wildlife).

Walk ¼ mile back down the entrance road (past the attendant's booth at the four-wheel drive entrance road) and turn left onto the sandy road along the marsh's edge. You'll see two nonchemical methods of insect control stretching across the marsh. The raised wooden boxes attract greenhead (horse) flies, which enter from the bottom, become trapped, and die. The bird houses attract tree swallows which devour flying insects.

Although your pace slows in heavy sand, this is an ideal area to look for animal signs. An animal track book will help you identify deer, rabbits, and the host of other animals that frequent the area.

After approximately ¾ of a mile you reach a large orange sign pointing left to Trail #1. Disregard the sign and continue straight as the trail curls along the marsh's edge. Orange markers guide your way. Watch for them at narrow forks (most of which rejoin quickly in any case).

After passing a small island of trees on the right, the road heads for a high, brush-covered dune and suddenly veers right around it. The setting is primitive and isolated.

Distance (round trip): 4.8 miles

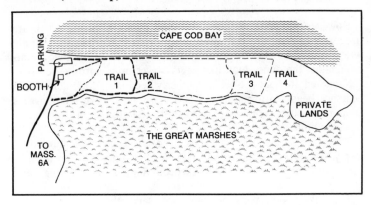

Turn north from Mass 6A at the sign for Sandy Neck Beach, 7.1 miles east of the Sagamore/Sandwich line and 2 miles west of the junction of Routes 6A and 149 in Barnstable. Pay the $7.00 fee, follow signs to the parking area, and read your copy of the Sandy Neck rules. Walk only on the trails to protect this fragile environment. Wind and water erode the dunes; only vegetation seems able to stabilize the sand.

Cedars and wild roses thicken the trailside ahead. This is an ideal spot to rest in the shade and scan the marsh for bird activity.

The way winds between two dwellings near the marsh, passes another to the left, and reaches the sign for Trail #2 after 2¼ miles. Go left between towering dunes. Turn left again onto Beach Road, which parallels the ocean. Walking becomes easier atop the beach's pebbles and packed sand. A 1-mile walk along the beach brings you to the exit for Trail #1. If you're still feeling fresh, go left here and travel 1¼ miles back to your car. For a quicker return, continue straight for ¼ of a mile to the parking area.

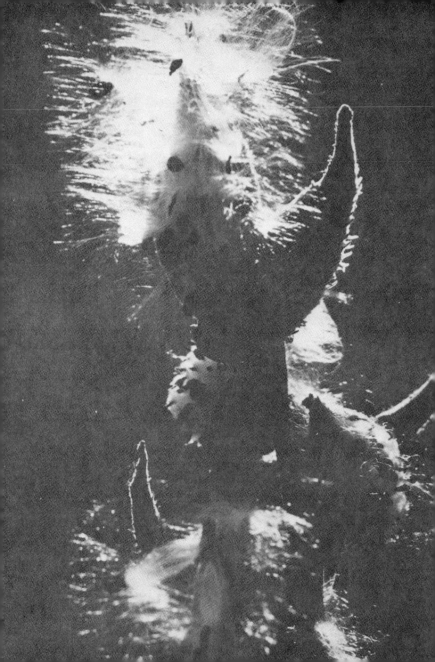

7. Yarmouth Nature Trails

A wheel-shaped herb garden introduces you to the Historical Society of Old Yarmouth's Nature Trails. Rosemary (signifying remembrance) rises from the center: Each herb in the garden is in memory of a former patron of the Society.

Indians originally called this area Mattacheset, meaning "old or planting lands by the borders of the water." Here they planted beans, pumpkins, and corn in natural and manmade clearings. Deer and smaller game filled the forests while ponds provided habitats for fish and waterfowl. There is little wonder that this naturally rich region was one of the first to be appropriated by white men.

Anthony Thacher, one of the three founders of Yarmouth, selected 156 acres of the best land for himself. He eventually paid the Indians with coats, breeches, hoes, hatchets, and metal kettles. Though Thacher descendants distinguished themselves in both the town and the larger world, they retained a love for the original land. In the early 1970s, a Thacher relative donated the present 50-acre woodland tract to the Historical Society.

The sandy trail begins to the left of the wheel-shaped herb garden. It quickly branches left and follows a grassy swath cut through open fields. The way leads into a quiet area forested with pitch pine, the Cape's most common pine. It generally grows on poor soils and can withstand strong winds and salt spray.

Oaks begin to mix with the pines. Delicate, pink lady's slippers dot the trailsides at ground level. A member of the orchid family, the flower can be easily identified by the singular, puffed-out, pink petal resembling the toe of a slipper. Two oval leaves from 6 to 8 inches long grow from the base of the stalk. Each plant has only one flower and one stem. Laws prohibit the picking of these flowers.

The stillness of the young oak forest might be broken by rustlings in the leaves: possibly from a chipmunk or squirrel, but more probably from a rufous-sided towhee. Its unmistakable call is a slurred *chewink*. The large size (up to 8 inches), dark heads, rusty sides, white bellies, and large white spots at the corners of the long, rounded tails make them easily identifiable. Towhees feed almost exclusively on the ground, persistently scratching away dead leaves to get at the insects underneath.

Distance: 1.25 miles

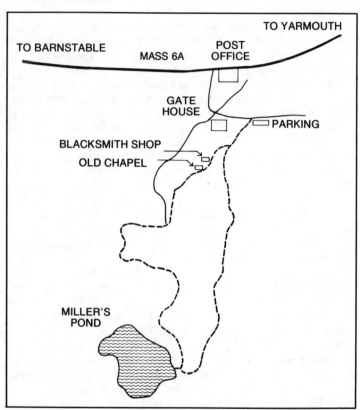

Turn south from Mass 6A onto the road leading behind the Yarmouth Port Post Office. Drive the short distance to the parking area near the gate house. A charge of $.50 for adults and $.25 for children covers the cost of admission and a descriptive pamphlet. Dogs must be on a leash.

Step down over the log-supported stairway to Miller's Pond. A short spur takes you to the water's edge. You may see animal tracks as well as frogs and turtles from this tiny observation area. Migrating waterfowl feed here in spring and fall.

Return to the main trail and follow it along the eastern shore. Pine odors engulf you as you weave your way through upland woods. Upon arriving at the old chapel and blacksmith shop, look right to the top of the hill. A massive purple beech dominates the skyline. Behind it is the skeletal shape of a rare Japanese geisha tree.

The path swings right and leads back to the parking area.

8. John Wing Trail

The natural creation of a salt marsh like the one skirting Wing's Island requires the life and death of a continuing succession of plants and marine life for hundreds of years. When a salt marsh is destroyed, it cannot be synthetically reconstructed through man's efforts. The town of Brewster's diligent efforts have preserved the natural loveliness of Wing's Island's 140 acres of upland, beach, and salt marsh.

The trail begins 100 feet west of the museum parking lot. An attractive signboard displays a map and capsule history of Wing's Island. Remember to check times for high tides before starting your hike because the causeway becomes flooded, particularly during spring tides.

Hike between a dense tree and shrub arborway before emerging into the openness of the salt marsh.

The short, soft salt marsh hay flourishing in the Wing's Island environs was of agrieconomic importance to Brewster's earlier residents. They piled the seasonal cuttings of marsh hay onto horse-drawn wagons and took them to the island itself where they laid the hay out to dry. Later, local farmers carted it away to store in their barns for cattle feed and mulch or to spread around the foundations of their homes for insulation.

After crossing the causeway, the trail reaches the more elevated island where thick vegetation narrows the way. Stay straight as a path enters from the right.

Keep left at two quick forks ahead as you head toward Quivett Creek Lookout. The path descends a bit, then arrives at a clearing at the marsh's edge. By remaining as quiet and hidden as possible, you may be able to watch stalking blue herons, acrobatic tree swallows, or hovering marsh hawks.

Retrace your steps to the most recent fork in the trail and go left toward Beach Lookout. Pitch pines shade both hikers and bearberry beneath them. Turn left as another trail joins from the right. Bear right at the next fork. You quickly reach Beach Lookout. From this vantage point you overlook the Brewster Flats and the beach in the distance.

Distance (round trip): 1.3 miles

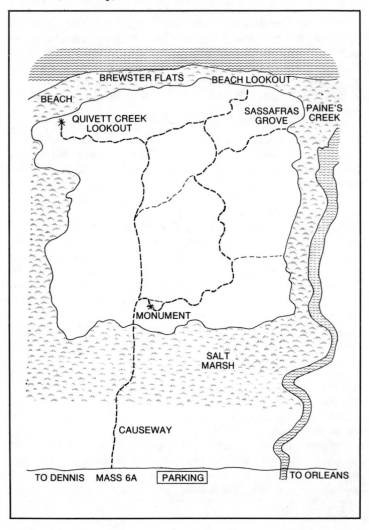

To reach the start of the trail on the north side of Mass 6A, drive 2.4 miles east of the intersection of Mass 134 and 6A in Dennis or 1.6 miles west of the intersection of Mass 137 and 6A in Brewster. Turn south into the John Wing Trail parking area (across the street from the Cape Cod Museum of Natural History). Remember—there are no public rest rooms at the John Wing Trail. Use the ones at the Brewster Police and Fire station 2 miles to the east. The John Wing Trail Guide, a fifteen-page pamphlet with descriptions keyed to the trail's interpretive markers, is available for $.50 at the Brewster Conservation Department or the Cape Cod Museum of Natural History.

Return to the most recent fork and stay straight. At the next fork go left, following the twisting trail that passes through a sassafras grove just before reaching the salt marsh edge. The untoothed sassafras leaves may be three-fingered, mitten- or egg-shaped. Spring blooming, greenish-yellow flowers and autumn-ripening, small, blue fruits aid identification. Settlers once fashioned barrels, posts, and dugout canoes from its durable, coarse lumber; they boiled the roots and bark to make sassafras tea, their "spring tonic."

Return to the most recent trail junction and go left, and left again at a quick fork. Staying straight at the fork ahead, you reach the stone marking the site of John Wing's home on the left. Just beyond, rejoin the original trail, turn left, and return to 6A.

9. North Trail
(Cape Cod Museum of Natural History)

An exciting, educational experience awaits you at the Cape Cod Museum of Natural History and its two trails: the North Trail (described here) and the South Trail (Walk #10). In addition to the trails, the museum provides natural history exhibits, live animal exhibits, films, lectures, classes for adults and children, and a fine environmental reference library. The museum is open (with the exception of Mondays in November, December, and January) from 9:30 A.M. to 4:30 P.M. Monday–Saturday and 12:30 P.M. to 4:30 P.M. on Sunday. Admission fees are adults, $2.50; children 6 to 14 years, $1.50; children under 6 years, free.

Enter the museum from the parking lot and be prepared to spend some time discovering new aspects of the natural world. Skeletons and stuffed specimens let you study the "ins and outs" of nature's inhabitants at close range. Dioramas and aquariums show display animals in naturelike settings. More than 5,000 books and periodicals about natural history fill the shelves of the museum's Clarence Hay Library. Special education programs take place in the auditorium, and the museum's store features an array of nature- and science-related gifts and books.

Pick up a guide to the North Trail at the museum and step outside from the museum's lower level. Numbered stations along this nature trail will help you identify much of the flora native to Cape Cod. Follow the path as it leads toward the marsh.

Watch immediately for wild roses. Not to be confused with the larger *Rosa rugosa* (wrinkled rose) which is abundant on the Cape, this dark pink, medium-sized rose has downward-curving thorns. Its flowers supply nectar for numerous insects.

The worn path leads along the marsh edge and reaches a short boardwalk. Walk out onto the large rock at the creek's edge for a better view of the area. The salt marsh cordgrass bordering the edges of the creek grows where salinity is high. It thrives in sand flats where its roots are submerged only half the time.

Just before the path dips into thicker growth, look left at the cattails. The slender, brown "cat's tail" is actually thousands of tiny female flowers topped by a lighter colored spike containing the male

Distance (round trip): .25 miles

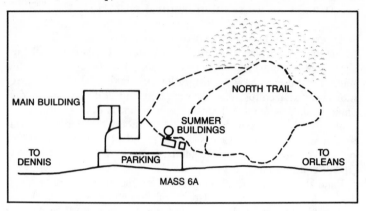

To reach the Cape Cod Museum of Natural History parking lot located on the north side of Mass 6A, drive 2.4 miles east of the intersection of Mass 134 and 6A in Dennis or 1.6 miles west of the intersection of Mass 137 and 6A in Brewster.

flowers. Cattails play vital roles within the marsh ecosystem. Muskrats eat their roots and stems and use them for construction materials; nesting birds and ducks seek their protective cover; and the ever-present red-winged blackbirds perch on their slender stems.

The path leads into thicker growth dominated by sumacs. Two kinds, both nonpoisonous, are evident here. Both have the typical sumac leaves made up of eleven or more toothed leaflets. Dwarf sumac has narrow wings along the leaf stalk between shiny leaflets; smooth sumac has hairless twigs and leafstalks and no wings.

The shady trail passes beneath a stand of tupelos and soon after reaches a bench where you can relax while looking out across the marsh. Turn left at the bench to follow the original path back to the museum.

10. South Trail
(Cape Cod Museum of Natural History)

During its passage through marshland and upland forest, the South Trail passes over Paine's Creek, a major migration route for alewives. Known as herring on Cape Cod, alewives make an annual spring migration from the ocean to inland rivers and streams to lay their eggs. A single female may carry as many as 60,000 to 100,000 eggs. Pilgrims sometimes depended on alewives as an extra food source and also used them to fertilize corn fields. Today, conservation measures keep alewives from being "overfished" and allow them to reach their spring spawning grounds.

Pick up your trail guide at the museum information desk.

From the parking lot you can see the South Trail's sign across Mass 6A. (You can walk directly from the parking lot, but you'll miss the numerous interesting features within the museum complex.)

Leave traffic sounds behind by stepping down over wooden steps into the cooling shade of shadbush and high bush blueberry. The path leads out to a marsh area and crosses a couple of wooden bridges over sluiceways.

These sluiceways once controlled the draining and flooding of the area to the right, which used to be a cranberry bog. Indians colored rugs and blankets with cranberry juice and flavored pemmican cakes and succotash with its tartness. Pilgrim women used the native fruit in cooking and cheered their wardrobes with the crimson pigment. Both Indians and the early settlers believed in the fruit's healing powers. Pequot Indians of Cape Cod treated poison arrow wounds with a cranberry poultice. They also imbibed the juice to calm their nerves. Rich in vitamin C, cranberries helped prevent scurvy among early American seamen voyaging to distant ports.

As you continue along the dike and into the woods ahead, watch for bird and animal life. You're apt to see deer, raccoons, muskrats, and a variety of birds. Animal tracks and "signs" (such as a discarded snake skin or droppings) will make this part of the walk all the more interesting.

Cross the large footbridge over Paine's Creek and enter the hardwood forest. The way leads through beech and tupelo groves before

39

Distance (round trip): .75 miles

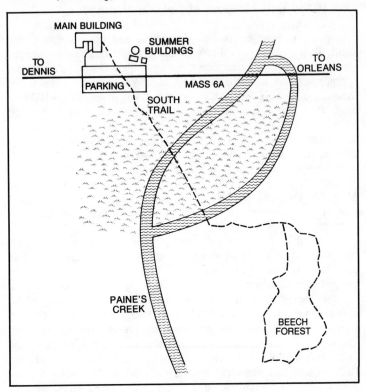

Follow directions in Walk #9 to the parking lot and pick up your trail guide at the museum desk.

bending right beside a split rail fence. Occasional orange, wooden arrows guide you around this circuit portion of the walk. Trailsides teem with poison ivy.

Nearing the end of the circuit, you arrive at a huge boulder sitting above a sand hole. It's fun to imagine Indians crouching behind this glacial erratic and looking out over the expanses of marsh for animal—or perhaps human—movement.

The path swings right to rejoin the original trail. Turn left and retrace your steps back to Route 6A.

11. Stoney Brook Mill Sites

Early Cape Cod settlers used both wind- and water-powered gristmills to grind corn for bread. When a stream, brook, or river with a year-round flow of water was discovered, a miller was granted water rights and free labor was provided to help build a gristmill. A dam was built, and the resulting millpond delivered a steady flow of water to move the wheel. Mills became centers of gossip and information, as every man stopped at one time or another to have corn ground.

You can watch corn being ground and packaged for sale at the Stoney Brook Gristmill from 2:00 P.M. to 5:00 P.M. on Wednesday, Friday, and Saturday during July and August. There is also an admission-free museum upstairs. At any time you can meander through the lovely grounds behind the mill. A millpond, dam, and herring run nestle within the tranquil, flowered setting.

A short, bricked-in path to the right of the mill leads up to the millpond. A split rail fence and sprawling honeysuckle vines surround this serene body of water. In spring and early summer the sweet-smelling honeysuckle blossoms perfume the air. Yellow and white trumpet-shaped flowers bloom from April through July; blackberries appear in August.

Look down into the still waters for sunfish activity. The 4-to-6-inch green sunfish spawn in colonies. Males push aside pond bottom vegetation and fan shallow, saucer-shaped nests in the sand with their fins. You'll see these residual signs of spawning activity throughout the year.

Wind your way up toward the larger pond and cross the footbridges. A sluicegate regulates the flow of water from the upper pond down to the mill itself.

Beyond the second footbridge, sounds of rushing water draw you beneath drooping weeping willows to the stone and cement sluiceway. In spring, you'll see thousands of tiny fish sashaying in the turbulent waters. These young alewives ("fry") hatch in the upper pond and, when about one-inch long, begin their journey down Stoney Brook to the ocean. In three to four years they will migrate back to spawn themselves.

Distance (round trip): .25 miles

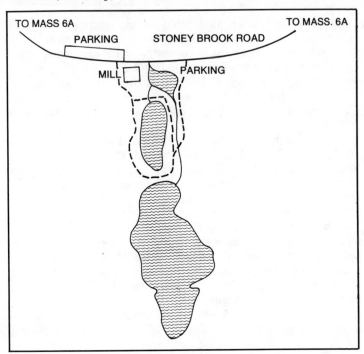

On Mass 6A in Brewster turn south onto Stoney Brook Road at the flashing yellow light located 3.3 miles east of the junction of 6A and 134 in Dennis and .7 miles west of the junction of 6A and 137 in Brewster. Drive .7 miles to the mill (on the left). Parking is available across the street.

This is a good spot to sit on a stone wall and enjoy the tranquil setting. The privacy of the secluded glen is highlighted by thick tree and shrub growth and broken only by the quieting sounds of rushing water and occasional croaking of frogs. A camera will help you remember the peaceful area.

At the fork ahead, go left to complete the loop around the lower pond. When back at this junction, go right, alongside the tumbling stream, toward the road.

You'll have a close-up view of the mill from across the small pond. This is a good vantage point from which to watch the water move the wheel as it, in turn, supplies the power for the grinding apparatus.

A few steps more will return you to Stoney Brook Road. Cross over and take the walk along the "ladders" where the herring come up in the spring. Go over the bridge and back to Stoney Brook Road.

12. Harding's Beach Trail

The more barren an area is, the more it attracts the horned lark. Each breeding pair appears to need some sparsely vegetated land within its territory. Thus, the scoured dunes along the Harding's Beach Trail are a favored horned lark haunt. When in flight, its white underparts contrast sharply with its black tail. The horned lark moves by walking, rather than hopping, across the sand. If disturbed it will fly only briefly before returning to earth.

The trail was established and is maintained by the Chatham Conservation Foundation, Inc., which also preserves other open areas, marshes, and uplands. A copy of *A Beachcomber's Botany*, with essays and comments by Dr. Loren C. Petry and illustrations by Marcia Norman, will add greatly to your enjoyment of this trail. Rights to the book were donated to the Chatham Conservation Foundation in 1972, and the proceeds, along with gifts and membership dues, enable the foundation to continue its valuable work.

Walk onto the wide sandy road that the trail follows for .6 miles. Numerous side trails short cut between salt spray rose and beach plum to the beach on the right.

The beach plum, a straggly, coastal shrub, bears purplish fruit used over the centuries to concoct sauces, preserves, pies, and jellies. Its white flowers bloom from April to June. Egg-shaped leaves, hairy buds, and velvety twigs will also help you identify this shrub.

Look left across the dunes to the salt marsh and Oyster River beyond. Fishermen grow and harvest oysters in this saltwater inlet; naturally flourishing bay scallops are also part of the bounty harvested there. (Chatham's early businesses included fishing, whaling, shipbuilding, and a saltworks; today, tourism is the major industry.)

Packed gravel makes the walking less ponderous. You top a long, low grade near station #13 and are treated to eye-stretching views of Oyster River, the salt marshes, and Stage Harbor to the left; look right to see Nantucket Sound and low, sandy Monomoy Island.

Just head, turn right and begin your return trip along the water's edge.

Your first ocean view may include a glimpse of the common tern's buoyant flight or rocketing dive. These birds fly parallel to the shore

Distance (round trip): 2.0 miles

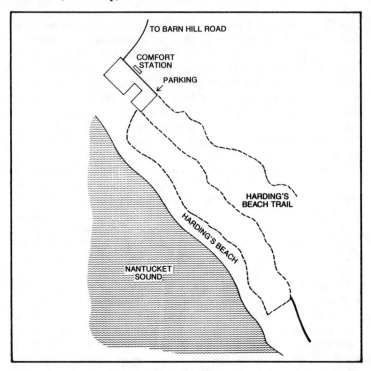

To reach the start of the trail, drive 1.7 miles west from the rotary in the center of Chatham on Mass 28. Turn left at the blinking light onto Barn Hill Road. After .4 mile, bear right at the fork onto Harding's Beach Road. Follow this to the parking lot entrance and pay the $3.00 per car fee for day use of the beach. Drive left along the edge of the parking lot past the comfort station into the smaller parking area. The trail begins at the far corner of this lot (near the beach).

with bills pointed downward, ever-scanning the shallows for schools of shiners. Black-capped and swallow-tailed, common terns plummet into the water to capture their prey. Diving terns are a positive sign for fishermen seeking bass and bluefish, for these bigger game fish feed on the shiners, too.

Take your shoes off, roll up pant legs, and enjoy a cooling walk in the shallows on your return route. Stop to examine the assortment of shells—and seaweed and driftwood—awash on the beach. Molting adult horseshoe crabs deposit their shells upon the shore. Actually, these animals are not crabs at all. Their closest relative became extinct 400 million years ago. This living fossil's closest relative is the spider. Though many bathers fear them, horseshoe crabs are harmless.

A second section of the trail begins at the northeast corner of the parking lot.

Complete your day at Harding's Beach with a swim or some surfcasting.

13. Fort Hill Trail

Natural and local history blend together as the Fort Hill Trail wanders over boardwalks through the Red Maple Swamp, crosses Skiff Hill, edges Nauset Marsh, ascends Fort Hill, and circles the Captain Edward Penniman House.

Pick up a Cape Cod National Seashore trail guide at the far end of the parking lot and step onto the wide trail. Take the left trail fork just ahead and descend over log-girdled steps. The path leads through meadows dotted with pines and cedars before entering the swamp.

Gray, weathered boardwalks curl through the lush vegetation. Narrow, scaly plates shingle the massive hulks of aged red maples. Cinnamon fern and wood fern proliferate in this damp, shady setting.

Ascend the paved path to Skiff Hill, where an octagonal, open-sided structure shelters Indian Rock. Nauset Indians used the boulder as a grinding rock, shaping bone points and fish hooks and sharpening tools and weapons on its varied surfaces.

The shortcut to the right leads back to the parking lot, but there's more to see ahead. Leaving Skiff Hill, the trail curves through a forest of pine and cedar. On the way to Fort Hill, scan Nauset Marsh, where egrets, great blue herons, or other waterfowl might be observed.

Ascend the sloping path toward Fort Hill past a large glacial boulder. Early settlers probably used the spike driven into the south side of this great rock to anchor a pulley for hauling loads of salt hay ashore. Rich in nutrients, the hay was used both as a garden mulch and as food and bedding for livestock.

Atop Fort Hill, the vista stretching before you includes Nauset Marsh straight ahead with the Atlantic beyond and Orleans Cove to the right. Samuel de Champlain considered establishing a settlement here in 1605 but was thwarted by unfriendly Indians and the shallowness of Nauset Harbor.

Before you reach the Captain Edward Penniman House, a 150-year-old house will appear to the right. It was built by the Knowles family who farmed land on both Fort and Skiff hills. The trail descends into a locust- and tree-filled hollow and swings around Captain Penniman's barn and house.

Distance (round trip): 1.5 miles

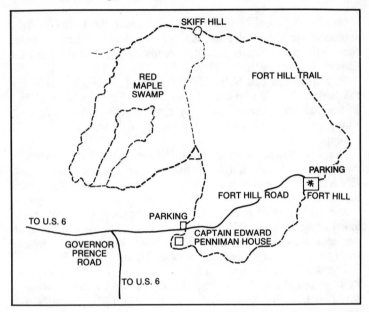

Drive north for 1.2 miles on Route 6 from the rotary junction of U.S. 6 and Mass 28 in Eastham to the Cape Cod National Seashore–Fort Hill sign. Turn right onto Governor Prence Road. At Fort Hill Road, turn right again and drive the short distance to the sign for the parking lot on the left.

In 1868 Captain Penniman had his house built in the French Second Empire style. It boasted a lead-lined rainwater cistern in the attic and indoor plumbing! A prosperous whaleship captain, Penniman wanted his nineteenth-century Victorian home to be the most elegant in Eastham. However, history records Captain Penniman's displeasure at the equally elegant taxes on his grand house.

The Fort Hill Trail ends by passing through the whalebone archway across the road from the parking lot. Such gateways date back to prosperous Cape Cod whaling days. Although Nantucket and New Bedford are probably the best known ports, whaling actually began on the Cape. The first whalers were idle farmers who discovered the magnificent mammals washed up on beaches in late fall and winter. Shore whaling gradually led to deep sea whaling, with cruises sometimes lasting four years.

14. Buttonbush Trail

How much do you really "see" while walking in the outdoors? Do you take time to stop and smell the flowers? Do you feel a tree's smooth or deeply furrowed bark? Are you in tune with forest sounds? A walk along the Buttonbush Trail will help you gain a stronger appreciation for the environment we so often take for granted. Close your eyes and open wide your other senses while walking this 1/4-mile route.

The Buttonbush Trail was designed for blind persons. A guide rope edges the narrow path. Two-inch plastic discs around the rope signal the presence of signposts, while pieces of garden hose remind you to step cautiously ahead. The signposts encourage you (in both braille and large print) to stop often, touch, listen, and smell.

For those who notice, contrasting surfaces pass underfoot. Your feet will pound jarringly onto hard-packed sand, crunch over soft pieces of shredded red cedar, resound dully atop a raised boardwalk, and slap harshly against tough macadam. Log steps make walking easier in steeply pitched sections.

Be prepared for sudden temperature changes. The comfort of a shaded path is quickly forgotten as you walk out into the sun's blazing heat. Returning just as rapidly to the refreshing coolness of a covered trail helps you appreciate the sun's strength and the forest's protection.

Pitch pine and red cedar, as well as other trees and shrubs, await your touch and smell. Also, listen for the sounds of pond activity. You might hear the liquid call of a red-winged blackbird or the sudden plop as a frog leaps to deeper, protective water. While sitting motionless in warm shallows, frogs absorb the sun's heat and use it to accelerate their "cold-blooded" body functions.

The path nears Nauset Road. Did you really "hear" the automobiles? Listen for the clicking of chains and gears and the soft whirring of tires as the path swings right to parallel a bicycle trail.

Your final steps slap onto macadam as the trail slopes down toward the starting point.

Distance (around loop): .25 miles

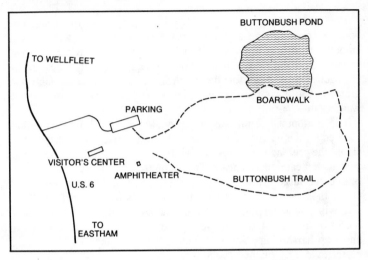

Turn east from U.S. 6 in North Eastham into the large parking lot at the Cape Cod National Seashore's Salt Pond Center. The Buttonbush Trail begins at the yellow guide rope to the left of the amphitheater. The path dips into cool, shaded woodlands, skirts the edge of a freshwater pond, and climbs over log steps during its circular route.

15. Nauset Marsh Trail

The Nauset Marsh Trail leads you through two distinctly different areas along its pleasant loop route. It first dips down to wind along the shorelines of Salt Pond and Nauset Marsh, then rises to weave through gentle, rolling countryside filled with beach plums, bayberries, and cedars. Overlooks encourage you to pause and reflect upon expansive, water-filled views, while shifting tides and abundant animal life invite you to explore actively the shoreline community.

Walk left of the Visitor's Center, down through the amphitheater, to the start of the trail. Descend the log steps to the cove and bear left along the wide trail edging the salt pond. Once a freshwater pond formed by receding glaciers, Salt Pond is connected to Nauset Marsh by a narrow channel. Daily tides enrich the pond and make it an ideal habitat for marine life.

A wooden boardwalk allows you to skirt the cove without getting wet. Along the water watch for the quick movements of a green heron. It has a gray back, reddish-brown neck and head, white throat, and bright orange legs. With head scrunched down on its shoulders, this small heron makes scurried explorations of the shallows. When in position, it leans forward, stalks slowly, and suddenly darts its bill into the water. If your patience matches that of this masterful fisherman, you'll soon see a small fish clasped between its bill.

A fork in the trail allows you to continue along the shore route or take a path up over log steps (they rejoin a short distance ahead). As you reach the marshy area next to the inlet connecting Nauset Marsh and Salt Pond, a wooden footbridge provides an ideal spot to watch for aquatic life. Look down into the shimmering water. Chances are you'll see crabs, small fish, barnacles, or horseshoe crabs.

Ascend log steps to the overlook and benches. Relax and enjoy the far-reaching views across Nauset Marsh.

Salt breezes and sea smells accompany you as you resume the walk. Cross more log steps and step onto soft, spongy masses of salt hay. Continued aquatic explorations will surely lead to countless broken clam shells, attesting to the ingenuity of great black-backed and herring gulls. Leaving the water's edge, ascend the sweeping

Distance (around loop): 1.2 miles

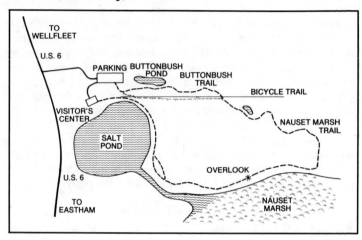

See Walk #14 (Buttonbush Trail) for directions to the Salt Pond Visitor's Center.

path to the left. As you crest a small rise, gaze back across Nauset Marsh.

Spire-shaped trees dot the rolling landscape as you weave in and out of cedars on the easy-to-follow trail. The path gradually descends to a tiny, tree-choked pond before rising again to wind through slender, candlelike eastern red cedars. Quick twists and turns speed you through the tree-lined maze.

Cross the macadam bicycle trail and step into thick groves of black locust trees. The rough, dark gray bark of these trees is broken into branching ridges. Because the wood is strong, hard, and resistant to decay, black locusts are often used as fenceposts. However, this tree was introduced to the Cape because it adds nitrogen to the soil, thereby helping change worn-out fields to fertile land.

Step out of the locust trees and cross the short, tarred road. Bear right at the Nauset Marsh Trail sign and descend the log steps. Follow the Buttonbush Trail's boardwalk back to the parking area.

16. Wellfleet Bay Wildlife Sanctuary

Wellfleet settlers reaped wealth from the sea through whaling and oystering until the British blockade during the Revolutionary War ruined their economy. Desperate bartering with England and France restored the town's prosperity, but the Embargo Act of 1807 interrupted trade once again. Despite these economic disasters, Wellfleet's resourceful seamen not only persisted but prospered. By 1850, only Gloucester surpassed Wellfleet in mackerel and cod catches. The Wellfleet oyster beds were New England's richest. Today that era has passed and tourism provides most of the income for the town. At the Wellfleet Bay Wildlife Sanctuary you have the opportunity to explore the area's natural history.

Information and trail guidebooks are available at the office (open 9:00 A.M. to 5:00 P.M. daily). Walk left from the parking area to the sign for the Goose Pond Trail. Shortly after starting your walk you'll pass Silver Spring Brook on the left. Silt and plant debris are gradually filling up the shallow pond formed by the brook's dam. Side paths poke through pond-edged greenery allowing chances to glimpse pond life.

As you emerge from the pines, a vista across marshlands to the bay unfolds. Wild lupine abounds in the sandy soil edging the trail. Note its pealike blue flowers and radiating leaves consisting of seven to ten segments.

After approaching Goose Pond the path swings right. A small blind for observing and photographing wildlife is set on the pond's left shore.

The trail continues past Goose Pond, crossing a wooden boardwalk. Go right at the fork beyond the pond. As the main trail reaches a small cabin on the left, a secondary loop trail branches right to Try Island. Time a side trip to Try Island carefully or you may be stranded; at the time of the vernal and autumnal equinoxes, high tide inundates the entire marsh (with the exception of the island).

Continuing its loop around to the left, the main trail passes a dugout building on the right. Tree swallows frequently nest in the bird houses set atop poles along here. These birds are completely white underneath and are the only green-backed swallows com-

Distance (round trip): 1.5 miles

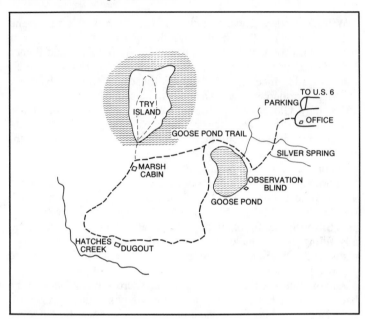

Soon after crossing from Eastham into Wellfleet on U.S. 6, watch for the blue and white Massachusetts Audubon Society sign on the left. Turn in and follow signs into the sanctuary. For those not members of the society there is an admission charge: $3.00 for adults; $1.50 for children and seniors.

monly seen in the east. Their swooping aerial acrobatics and wide mouths aid them in capturing enormous quantities of insects. In cold weather they feed on bayberries.

Wintering eastern bluebirds and yellow-rumped warblers also eat bayberries, which are actually wax-covered nutlets. Candles are made from its waxy coating. When crushed or baked in the sun, the leaves give off a pungent aroma; bayberry's generic name, *Myrica,* comes from the Greek word for perfume.

The Goose Pond Trail finishes its loop at the fork just west of Goose Pond. Turn right onto this familiar part of the trail and follow it to the parking lot.

17.   Atlantic White Cedar Swamp Trail

Both natural and historical features attract one to the Cape Cod National Seashore's Marconi Area.

Guglielmo Marconi built his wireless station on the crest of the high dunes rimming this section of the Great Beach. On January 18, 1903, the station's radio transmitted the first telegraphic message across the Atlantic to Poldhu, in Cornwall, on the southern tip of England.

Pounding breakers have reclaimed the sandy bluffs on which the station once stood. However, excellent displays, photographs, three-dimensional models, and an audio program within the Marconi Station pavilion commemorate the people and places associated with the historic event.

Include, also, a visit to the nearby Observation Platform in your trip to the Marconi Area. Its 360-degree view takes in the head of Black Fish Creek, which is the narrowest point on Cape Cod.

A sign on the left side of the parking lot marks the beginning of the trail. The wood-chip-covered path winds through scrub oaks and pitch pine. Bearberry forms dense evergreen carpets several yards across and a few inches high through here. In mid-May, note its waxy-white, urn-shaped flowers; pink coloring edges the flowers' small mouths. Dull red berries last into November.

Gnarled pitch pine archways deposit cushiony, needle carpets on the path as the trail bends around an oddly misshapen tree. Log steps offer firm footing as you climb and descend amongst increasingly taller and thicker oak trees.

The trail swings left and leads through the American White Cedar Swamp via an elevated boardwalk. Stay left at the fork ahead, the right fork is an alternate—but much shorter—route through the swamp. This swamp began ten to twelve thousand years ago when glaciers retreated, leaving huge blocks of rock and soil-covered ice. When the ice blocks melted, the rocks and soil settled to form kettle holes.

Take time to enjoy the unusual swamp flora and (if you're lucky) fauna. Of course, the swamp's namesake is also its most imposing feature. Atlantic white cedar wood has been prized for centuries for its resistance to insects and disease. Indians fashioned canes from its

67

Distance (round trip): 1.25 miles

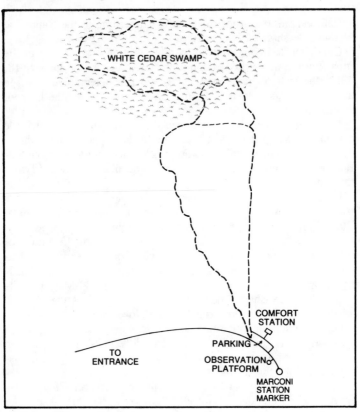

Turn right into the Marconi Station Area at the traffic light on Route 6, South Wellfleet, 5.2 miles north of Salt Pond Visitor Center, Eastham. Following signs for Marconi Site and White Cedar Swamp Trail, drive 1.1 miles to the Marconi Site parking lot.

light, rot-resistant wood; American revolutionaries made gunpowder from white cedar charcoal. Cedar chests have preserved generations of clothing from moths and mildew.

Shortly after the alternate route enters from the right, you leave the boardwalk and the cool, humid cedar swamp behind. After climbing a short, gradual, sandy grade, swing left onto a wider trail. This is the Old Wireless Road, the original access route to Marconi's station.

Walk over the soft sand up this long, gradual incline to where you rejoin the wood chip path. Turn left to the parking lot.

18. Great Island Trail

The arduous Great Island Trail requires sun hats, drinking water, sturdy hiking shoes, a fit body, and an early morning start to avoid the intense midday summer sun. (You'll also need to schedule the midpoint of your hiking time to coincide with low tide if you wish to explore Jeremy Point.) Yet the rewards are many, from glimpses of the feisty fiddler crab to the "natural high" that Jeremy Point's wind-and-wave-swept wildness gives you.

The Great Island Trail begins to the left of the parking area and curls down between pitch pines to the mouth of the Herring River. Crunching salt hay underfoot, bear right at the water's edge. Early settlers fed their cattle nutrient-rich salt hay; current settlers still use the hay as a garden mulch.

Walking along the sandy road bordering the tidal flat, you'll see animal signs etched in the sand. Gulls leave alternating "walking" tracks, while sideways-moving fiddler crabs leave lacy tracings. These burrowing crabs dig subterranean communities up to three feet long in the drier parts of salt marshes and sandy beaches. Only the male sports the outsized, singular claw for which the animal was named. Though the claw is used primarily in mating season battles, males seem to enjoy waving them threateningly at passing hikers.

Bear left at the base of the grass-and-shrub-covered dunes ahead, still edging the tidal flat. Beyond the vehicle barricade ahead, bear right. (The path continuing straight leads to the old Smith's tavern site.)

Marsh pea flourishes to the sides of the now narrower trail. Clusters of three to ten purplish flowers bloom from the ends of long stalks. Each blossom's lower lip is lighter in color than the turned back upper lip. The plant's paired leaflets are an appropriate pea-green shade.

As the grade increases you enter a wooded area where pitch pines offer a welcome respite from blazing sun.

After 1³/₄ miles of walking, a semicircular path leads left to a small memorial bearing a quote by Governor William Bradford of Mayflower fame. Rejoin the main trail and continue to the crest of a small rise for a view across grass-covered dunes to Cape Cod Bay. Descend to Middle Meadow, another low, marshy area. Once again,

Distance (round trip): 8.4 miles

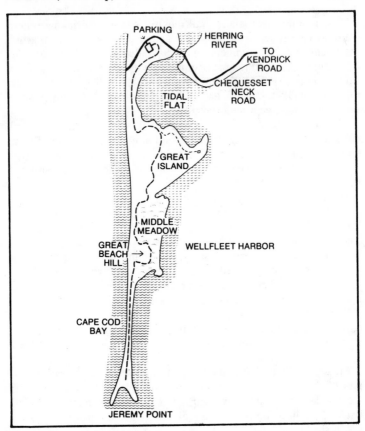

Follow signs from U.S. 6 to Wellfleet Center and Chequesset Neck. Just beyond the Town Pier, bear right onto Kendrick Road. Drive 2.3 miles and turn left at the sign for Great Island. The parking lot closes midnight to 6:00 A.M.

you'll have to dodge the skittling fiddler crabs as they erupt from or disappear into their burrows.

After skirting the edge of the meadow, the trail bears right briefly then swings left up over dunes. Look back from the top of this rise for a northerly view across Cape Cod Bay. On a clear day you can spot the Pilgrim Monument in Provincetown.

A sign at the fork ahead directs you left. Enjoy this cool walk through more pitch pines. Another expansive view of Cape Cod Bay appears just before you descend to a third marshy area.

The path makes a looping bend to the right before reaching a sign pointing to Jeremy Point. (If weary, head back now.) The 1.2 mile Jeremy Point trail begins atop low, grass-covered dunes. But quickly swing down onto the beach, take off your shoes, and enjoy a mile of solitary beachcombing as you follow this curling sand spit into the sea.

Return via the same route.

PILGRIM SPRING

Near here on November 16, 1620, the Pilgrims, on their initial, "Discoverie" trip up Cape Cod from Provincetown, found their first fresh water. The Pilgrims' chronicle, *Mourt's Relation* (1622), relates the tale:

..."sat vs downe and drunke our first *New England* water with as much delight as euer we drunke drinke in all our liues."

Although location of the spring has been contested by some historians, these springs from this spot have been checked and they match the _____

19. Pilgrim Heights Trail

Although the Pilgrims selected Plymouth Harbor as their final stopping place in America, they initially dropped anchor in Provincetown Harbor in November 1620. While the women stayed aboard ship, Pilgrim men rowed ashore to explore and search for food and water. They discovered water at a spring in North Truro and spent their second night in the New World beside it. A quote from the Pilgrim's chronicle, "Mourt's Relation," helps us appreciate both our ancestors' writing style and their joy at tasting their first New England water: "Sat us downe and drunke our first New England water with as much delight as ever we drunke drinke in all our lives."

The needle-covered path leads through thick, pitch pine woods. Sandy in spots, the trail winds out into open areas and back beneath gnarled pines.

The path eventually emerges from the low, scrubby woods onto an overlook. You gaze out over Salt Meadow (a freshwater marsh) to sand dunes and the Atlantic Ocean beyond. Migratory waterfowl use Salt Meadow as a sheltered resting area during their semiannual excursions. In spring, parent waterfowl lead armadas of young across the marsh's placid waters.

Great blue heron are one of the types of migratory waterfowl that may be observed in the Salt Meadow. This long-legged wading bird stands up to 38 inches high and has up to a 70-inch wingspread. In flight, its neck and head fold back, wings flap surprisingly smoothly, and legs trail straight out behind. When hunting for small fish and frogs, the heron walks slowly through shallows or stands poised with head hunched on shoulders before quickly thrusting its lethal bill underwater.

The trail steps down over a series of log-supported steps and narrows as it passes thick bramble patches. This area provides an ideal habitat for cottontail rabbits, although you will only seldom see these furry hoppers. If lucky, you might surprise one crouched in the middle of the path with ears up, nose twitching, and eyes wide with watchfulness before it bounds away.

The trail turns sharply right here and leads gradually uphill through thick forests. Leveling out, it leads through a picnic area and reaches the picnic area parking lot.

Distance (around loop): .75 miles

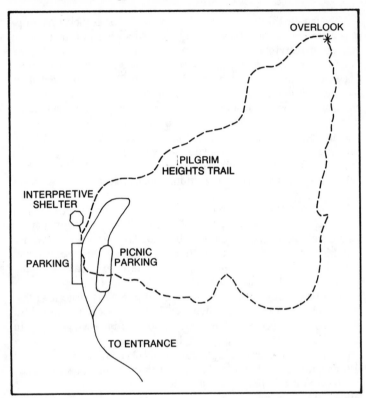

To reach the trail's start, proceed 2.1 miles north on U.S. 6 from the junction of Mass 6A and Route 6 in North Truro. Turn right at the sign for Pilgrim Heights area and follow the arrows to the parking area near the Interpretive Shelter. The trail begins between the far end of the parking area and the shelter.

Continue straight across this parking area and follow the trail up to the parking area near the Interpretive Shelter.

20. Small's Swamp Nature Trail

No other birds give us that wild thrill we feel while watching the wide, soaring circles or the plummeting attack of a hawk or osprey. From vantage points along Small's Swamp Nature Trail, you can scan Salt Meadow and have a good opportunity of spotting a marsh hawk and of observing its gliding, hovering search for prey. A long tail, prominent white rump, and long, rounded wings held above the horizontal aid identification of this harrier. Though much less common, you might also see the osprey (fish hawk). A black band on each leg and crooks in their wings offer the best field marks for these hawks. They often hover 50 to 150 feet above the water, then plunge to seize fish at or just below the surface.

Just beyond the Interpretive Shelter, the trail begins by descending through a pitch pine forest. Spring breezes gently rock the delicate white star flowers edging the trail at ankle level.

After bearing sharply left along a wooden fence, you reach a fork in the trail. Walk left here over logged steps. Switchback to the left and continue your steep descent into the kettle.

A dawn or twilight walk might acquaint you with some of this area's residents: red and gray squirrels, skunk, raccoon, red fox, white tail deer, and box turtles.

At the bottom of the kettle, the more level path passes between thickets of poison ivy and swamp azalea. Swamp azalea's white, vase-shaped flowers bloom May through August. This medium to tall shrub has leaves that are glossy green above and green to white beneath.

A snow fence borders the base of a towering dune to the left. High bush blueberries offer sweet, thirst-quenching fruit in mid-summer. Songbirds, mourning doves, pheasants, and ruffed grouse feast on the blue to blue-black fruit.

Ahead the trail bends right past areas favored by red-starts, northern orioles, and rufous-sided towhees. A small, swampy area lies to the right.

Swing right again at the next bend and mount a long series of log steps which aid your ascent from the floor of the kettle. Gray catbirds squeakily serenade you from the low trees to either side of the trail. Bearberry hugs the pathsides.

Distance (around loop): .75 miles

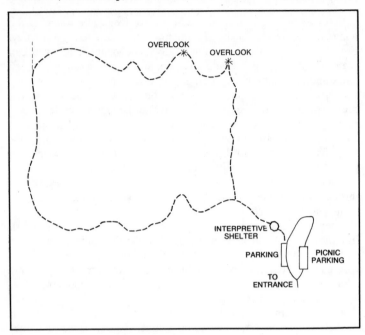

To reach the start of the trail, see the directions in Walk #19 (Pilgrim Heights Trail).

Soon you reach the summit of a glacial headland and the first of two Salt Meadow overlooks with promised chances to glimpse a bird of prey. Wind ruffles the channeled waters of this (surprisingly enough) freshwater marsh. Thomas Small and son Warren selected this kettle site for its protection from the wind and farmed the surrounding area for years. Their major crop was salt hay.

Move on to the second Salt Meadow overlook and spend some time looking, listening, and inhaling fragrant ocean breezes.

Switchback sharply right and walk gradually upward through a pitch pine and scrub oak forest. After a brief walk you reach a junction with the original trail. Bear left and return to the Interpretive Shelter.

21. Beech Forest Trail

Shaded paths bordered by lush greenery await you at the Beech Forest Trail in the Cape Cod National Seashore's Province Lands Area. Much of this gradual walk follows the edges of two freshwater ponds; the rest is a ramble through beech forests.

Thriving forests once blanketed this northernmost tip of Cape Cod. However, early settlers from Europe showed little concern for preserving the natural resources. Clear cutting, overgrazing, and forest fires obliterated the native forests and meadows. Shifting dunes and windblown sand threatened to destroy the Province Lands settlements. In the 1800s strict conservation controls and beach grass plantings began to stabilize the dunes' movement.

The Beech Forest Trail leads right from the end of the parking area. The way swings left, passing clumps of the aptly named wrinkled rose with its heavily wrinkled leaves and hairy stems. Occasionally, the large, deep pink blossoms fade to white. On long voyages, Colonial seamen ate the wrinkled rose hips to prevent scurvy. Today Cape Codders make rose hip jelly.

Trees and shrubs hug the path as you pass a pond and cross over a small wooden footbridge. In sight of the water, search for turtles, ducks, and wading birds. Watch more closely for the movements of water striders, dragonflies, and whirligig beetles.

The footing along the main trail softens as the sand gets deeper.

Several different species of pine grow here. You can identify pitch pine by its bunches of three needles and its dead cones still on the branches. Scotch pine has rust-colored bark and bundles of two short, twisted needles, 1/2 to 3 inches long. Austrian pine has longer needles (up to 6 inches), also grouped in twos.

Oaks mix with the pine as the trail goes past rising sand hills and reaches a fork. The path to the left continues around the pond. Go right for a walk through the beech forest. These handsome trees have smooth, light gray bark and prominently toothed, elliptical leaves.

After about 1/4 mile the way turns sharply left and climbs a sandy embankment. Logs cross the trail creating a series of rustic steps.

The path labors downward over more steps and winds past dunes to the pond's other side. Shadows in the sand reflect the needled pitch pine branches above.

Distance (around loop): 1 mile

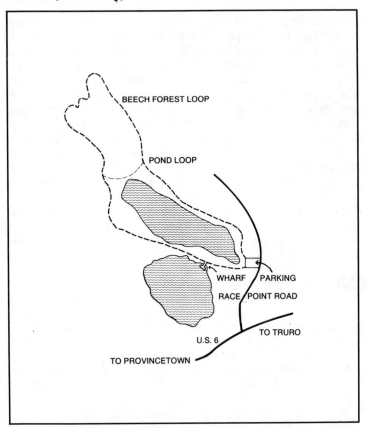

Turn north from U.S. 6 in Provincetown at the traffic light on Race Point Road. Continue ½ mile to the Beech Forest Trail parking area on the left.

To the left, pond lilies almost smother the water's surface. Their thick yellow flowers become erect and bloom atop the large, protective leaves in late spring and early summer.

Ahead to the right a plank wharf protrudes into a smaller pond. Linger here in the sun and enjoy the isolated beauty. Wind and animal sounds keep you company.

Retrace your steps on the wharf and turn right to return to the parking area.

Martha's Vineyard

Ferries from Woods Hole, Falmouth
Heights (summer only), and Hyannis
(summer only) will get you to Martha's
Vineyard, but advance reservations are
a must if you are traveling during
summer months with a car or bike (the
standby lane is a gamble, at best).

22. Indian Hill

Eye-stretching 360-degree views from the firetower atop 262-foot Indian Hill are yours for the climbing. From the firetower, the highest vantage point on Martha's Vineyard, you can look north across Lambert's Cove and Makoniky Head to Woods Hole. East and southeast sun winks off planes at Martha's Vineyard Airport. Gay Head cliffs and lighthouse are visible to the southwest. Look west and northwest out across the Elizabeth Islands to Newport, Rhode Island. On a clear day you'll spot the tops of the Newport Bay Bridge.

An osprey (fish hawk) might give you a rare and special thrill and fly by the tower on its way to or from a fishing expedition at Tisbury Great Pond. This bird-of-prey's large eyeballs leave little space in his cranium for a brain. Yet this hawk shows ingenious intelligence in at least two instances: he carries his captured prey head forward, reducing wind resistance; and before his migration south, he reinforces his nest with fresh, green twigs to help it withstand harsh winter winds.

Sachem Josias gave the 1-mile-square parcel of land, including Indian Hill, in 1660 to be used as a praying town for Indian converts to Christianity. The Algonquin Indians knew it as *Manitouwattootan* (Christiantown). The praying town is located in West Tisbury, first dubbed *Tackhum-Min-Eyi* or *Takemmy*, Algonquin for "The Place Where One Goes to Grind Corn."

Walk across from the parking lot past the large stone marker. Pass through to the back of the burial ground and swing sharply left to the narrow trail leading toward Indian Hill. Huckleberry bushes pinch in from both sides and brush against your legs.

Listen for the high-pitched chirping of chipmunks through here. You might think the repetitive outbursts are a bird's call—unless you see the animal's unmistakable back stripes. They stuff their cheeks with amazing amounts of nuts, which they store in underground burrows for winter use. Although chipmunks are mostly terrestrial, we've seen them scamper up trees and even swim across a river.

At the small clearing beneath the telephone lines bear left and then go right onto the dirt road ahead. Passing beneath the telephone lines, the road bends right, climbs a short, moderately steep grade, and arrives at the firetower. Climb up for the promised panorama.

Distance (round trip): .5 miles

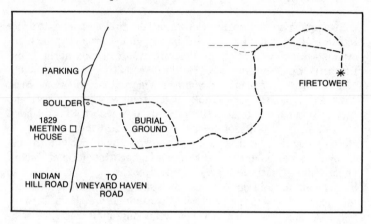

From Vineyard Haven drive or bike west on Vineyard
Haven Road, following signs for West Tisbury, Chilmark,
and Gay Head. After. 4.3 miles Lambert's Cove Road joins
from the right. Continue west on Vineyard Haven Road for
100 yards and turn right onto Indian Hill Road. Travel .5
miles to a crossroads and turn right. Another .5 miles will
bring you to the Indian Hill parking area on the left.

Retrace your steps down the road from the tower and watch for a
path leading left. You might want to take this path to vary your
return route. It follows the power lines down to where they cross the
road below. Rejoining the dirt road, walk a short distance and swing
left onto your original route through the burial ground to the parking
area.

23. Cedar Tree Neck Sanctuary

Your outdoor tastebuds will enjoy a delectable, full-course experience at Cedar Tree Neck Sanctuary. The largest sanctuary under the stewardship of the Sheriff's Meadow Foundation, Cedar Tree Neck offers walks over varied terrain through woods, along ponds, and to the ocean. Birdlife and mushrooms abound.

There is no charge for enjoying Cedar Tree Neck Sanctuary, but donations are accepted and used for its upkeep as well as that of other Sheriff's Meadow Foundation properties. A large, mapped signpost near the parking lot shows the trail system and lists walking times. If you don't have the several hours this area (and you) deserves, base your explorations on the suggested times. (Swimming is not allowed, and the gate closes at 5:00 P.M.)

Follow the Red Trail's narrow, shady, meandering path. Red blazes on trees guide you over a small brook to a fork (both routes rejoin shortly). Low scrub growth and taller oak trees fill the trailsides.

Descend to the junction with the Yellow Trail and bear right across another brook. As your pace slows in deeper sand, you'll step into the open and see sand dunes with Vineyard Sound beyond. Cedar Tree Neck Pond is to the right.

Walking becomes more laborious in deep sand as you follow red-painted sticks between dunes and pond. At the far corner of the pond, the trail forks to form a pleasant loop. Bear left through low scrub growth, wildflowers, and sumac to the overlook atop a 30-foot bluff. A wooden bench encourages you to enjoy the expansive views across the sound and up and down Martha's Vineyard's coast. The seaside panorama reminds us of the northern California–Oregon coastline.

The loop trail continues beneath shady trees as it edges the pond. Watch and listen for the jet plane-like flight and raucous chattering of kingfishers through here.

If time permits, beachcomb awhile before returning to the junction with the Yellow Trail. Bear right across a gurgling brook and look for wildlife footprints in the mud.

Yellow blazes lead you gradually uphill through smooth-barked, steel-gray beeches. Ferns, mosses, and mushrooms line the trail, and birds chirp in the woods. The trail bends around Ames Pond.

Distance (round trip): 3.5 miles

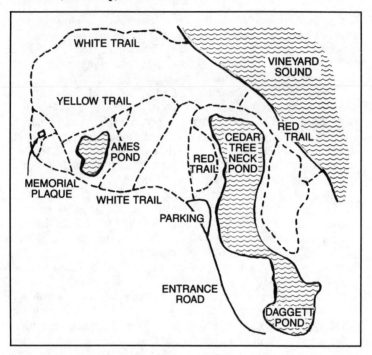

See Walk #22 for directions to Indian Hill Road. Follow Indian Hill Road 1.8 miles to the sign for Cedar Tree Neck Sanctuary. Go 1 mile on the narrow gravel road to the sanctuary entrance. Take the short road to the parking area. (Remember: The gate closes at 5:00 P.M.)

This small, secluded haven contains several wood duck houses. Watch for these beautiful, crested birds and listen for their whistling flight.

At the junction with the White Trail, bear right and follow the short steep path to a large hillside boulder. An inscribed plaque depicts the Alexander S. Reed Bird Refuge. Of the many birds observed here, one of the more unusual is the rufous-sided towhee. Watch for this fellow on the ground and in low bushes.

A variety of mushrooms dot the trail as it passes through taller trees before descending gradually to a damp, dark, spongy area. Cross the elevated catwalk and follow the sandy path to the shore. Views are more restricted here, but the crescent-shaped beach to the right invites walkers.

Return via the White Trail to the parking area.

24. Middle Road Sanctuary

Scattered clusters of rocks poking up through the earth atop a low knoll identify an Indian burial ground along the Middle Road Trail. Martha's Vineyard's Wampanoag Indians had subjected themselves to the English king and God by 1675 and had become Christians. As such, they not only believed they were superior to shamans and invulnerable to their sorcery, but they also began to bury their dead, as the white man did. Some of these Christian Indians gouged symbols depicting themes, hopes, or other statements on burial stones.

This pleasant walk begins as a flat, grassy trail surrounded by oak trees. Oak trees continue to proliferate along the entire trail. After gradual ups and downs, the trail forks. Go left. When you begin to see the distant Atlantic Ocean through the trees, watch for the short, narrow path leading to the burial ground on the right. The Wampanoag Indians buried their dead in upright positions. The hiker is left to speculate about the placement of the stones in the burial ground. Do three stones side by side represent a family? Could a larger, more solitary stone mark the grave of a chief?

Return to the main trail. It descends Abel's Hill and passes a large, glacial boulder. Stone walls suddenly border the trail on the left and lead to a 90-degree turn to the right. Stop here and look left to numerous stone walls and the only remaining brick barn on Martha's Vineyard. (Do not trespass on this private property.) Early settlers cleared stones from their fields and used the stones to make walls for boundary markers and to build pens for their livestock.

Stone walls and briars line the trail as it continues past an old sand pit and turns sharply right. Becoming sandier amidst the ever-present oaks, the path descends gradually. A contemporary house brings you briefly back to civilization.

Following a sandy road, the trail passes more houses. Just before a brick house on the left, it turns sharply right and becomes a narrow path once again. The trail proceeds uphill, leaving the houses behind.

You may see wasps' nests hanging pendulously from trees along here. A female wasp makes the "paper" for her nest by chewing plant fibers or old wood. She then spreads the paper in thin layers to make cells where she will lay eggs. The nests found along this trail

Distance (round trip): 1.3 miles

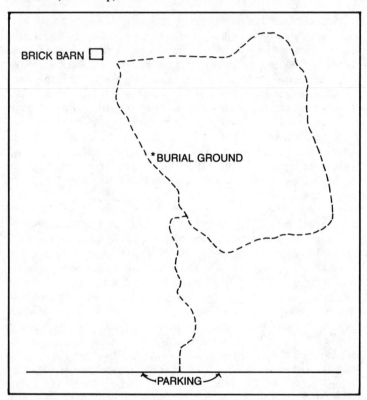

From Vineyard Haven, follow signs for West Tisbury, Chilmark, and Gay Head 7.4 miles to the First Congregational Church in West Tisbury. Turn right onto Music Street beside the church. Drive .5 miles and turn left onto an unnamed paved road. Travel .5 miles and watch for the Middle Road sanctuary sign on the left. Park on the side of the road.

are constructed of many cells covered by paper with a single hole for an entrance/exit. This design is typical of two types of wasps: hornets and yellow jackets.

Topping a hill, the trail passes to the right of several more houses before eventually turning sharply right and returning to wooded seclusion again. Gradual, uphill meanderings return you to the original fork. Bear left and return to your car.

25. Manuel F. Correllus State Forest

If you like strolling beneath towering pines, standing silently in the hushed silence and subdued hues of thick, closely bunched evergreens, and padding stealthily over trails layered with needles, put this hike on your *must* list. The nature trail's pine-filled forests engulf and dominate you during most of this pleasant woods walk. (The forest also features 12 miles of bike trails and 10 miles of horse trails.)

Continue down the forest road for 100 yards and swing right onto the nature trail. The wide grassy swath passes a sunken pond to the left and leads through rows of red pines. Unfortunately, red pines are dying out in this area due to a fungus infection. More appropriate species are being planted to replace these pines.

Reaching a wide fork, continue straight ahead. Scrub oaks temporarily replace the pines to the left. Soon the thick rows of pines resume their domination of both trailsides. Eastern white pines begin to mingle with the reds as the comfortable path swings sharply left and back again to the right.

White pines have 3-inch to 5-inch needles in bundles of fives. Young trees have smooth gray bark; older ones have dark, deep-furrowed bark. The largest conifer in the northeast, white pines once grew to heights of 200 feet and more. However, due to extensive lumbering, especially for house construction, these trees are seldom allowed to exceed 75 to 100 feet in height.

After following a long straight path, the way turns sharply left onto a grassier trail. As the pines thin out, blueberry bushes edge the trail.

Turn left at the next intersection (following the nature trail sign). Ahead, pines litter the path with cones and needles; the needles are so thick they feel like piles of hay underfoot. White pine cones are slender and 2 to 4 inches long; red pine cones are plumper and smaller.

Red squirrels may scold you from the protection of pine boughs. These industrious creatures are masters at gathering food. They will cut loose numerous nuts and cones in a single session, then gather them together for deposit in underground hideaways. They also will carry mushrooms up into trees and place them on limbs to dry.

Distance (round trip): 1 mile

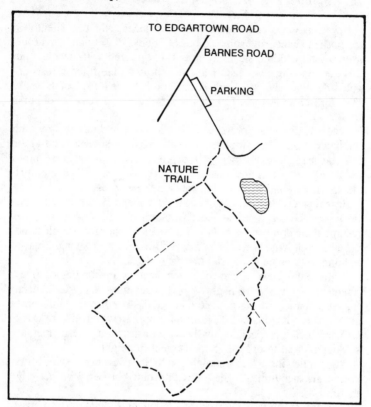

From Vineyard Haven follow signs for West Tisbury, Chilmark, and Gay Head for .4 miles. Turn left at the sign for Edgartown. Drive 2.2 miles and turn right onto Barnes Road. After .9 miles turn left at the State Forest sign. The parking lot is immediately on your left.

After crossing a wide, grassy path, the trail meanders through a white spruce forest. White spruces have four-sided, bluish-green needles arranged in compact spirals around nonhairy twigs (red and black spruces have hairy twigs). Cones are 1 to $2^{1}/_{2}$ inches long with thin, flexible scales. The tree's outer bark is an ash brown color.

The path swings right toward an old barn and left again. With the sunken pond visible through trees on your right, turn right at the next intersection and return to the parking area.

26. Felix Neck Wildlife Sanctuary

Interpretive pamphlets guide you over miles of trails through open fields and woodlands and along marshes, beaches, and small ponds at the Felix Neck Wildlife Sanctuary. An observation hut enables you to watch and identify a living collection of native waterfowl. From a photography blind you can observe or photograph wild ducks and geese. The visitor's center contains maps, booklets, exhibits, and a library with a good ecological and environmental reference collection. Knowledgeable staff and volunteers will answer your questions.

In 1963, George Moffett, owner of the 200 acres that now make up the sanctuary, and two close friends formed the Martha's Vineyard Natural Historical Society. In 1967 the land was donated to the Massachusetts Audubon Society.

Walk from the far end of the parking lot through the trees to the visitor's center. Browse through this building before beginning your walk. When ready to stretch your legs, go left around the donation box to the Yellow Trail markers.

The flat, grassy path passes an open field and winds through a narrow wooded area. Rising onto walkalongs, it reaches a small semicircular pond. The blueberry bush-lined Shad Trail exits left here. Follow it to the small marshy strip at the edge of Major's Cove.

Return to the Yellow Trail and turn left through older, thicker woods. The alternately sandy and grassy path weaves in and out of wooded areas before arriving at a small weathered building. The Yellow Trail passes by the cabin and slithers between high bush blueberries. Poison ivy grows throughout this area and serves as a constant reminder to remain on the trails. At the end of the Yellow Trail you can see the sandy finger of Edgartown Beach across Major's Cove.

Retrace your steps to the cabin and take the trail that exits left from the circular road in front of it. This flat path leads to the photography blind. With or without camera or binoculars, you can observe wild waterfowl on Sengekontacket Pond.

Return to the circular road, swing left, and follow it to the Red Trail. Turn left again. Fresh sea breezes will brush your face as you walk out to the shore of Sengekontacket Pond once more. Try whistling *bob white* to the quail that enliven this area.

Distance (round trip): 1.75 miles

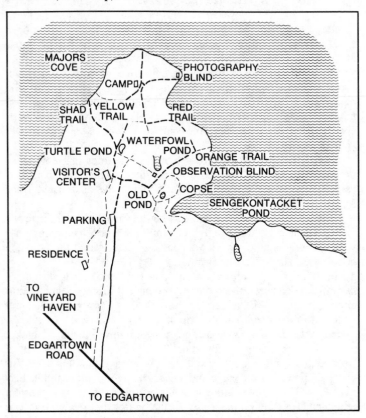

From Vineyard Haven, turn right (west) and follow signs for West Tisbury, Chilmark, and Gay Head for .4 miles. Turn left at the sign for Edgartown and go 4.6 miles to the sanctuary entrance's plain granite marker (on left). Turn left and go .7 miles on the sandy access road to the parking lot.

Turn right onto the Orange Trail and walk to the observation blind at the edge of Waterfowl Pond. Here you can watch flocks of native dabbling and diving ducks. Because the many types of captive waterfowl act as decoys and because the sanctuary is located on a migratory flyway, numerous species of wild waterfowl visit the pond each year.

Continue on the Orange Trail back to the visitor's center.

27. John Tuttle Sanctuary

The John Tuttle Sanctuary Trail was laid out in 1988. As the newest of the Sheriff's Meadow Foundation properties at that time, it represented another in the foundation's growing list of "forever wild" areas. By 1988 the foundation's properties were extensive enough to require the services of a full-time naturalist. The foundation grew, thanks to the dedicated efforts and leadership of founder Henry Beetle Hough and, later, his wife, Edith Blake.

This sanctuary offers a variety of natural features along its loop trail. The trail follows the gently rolling terrain, leading to both water and marsh views. Birders may have opportunities to view warblers and red-winged blackbirds.

The trail heads gradually uphill and swings left before passing a large depression on the right. It is all that remains of a barn built into the hillside many years ago. Just ahead, bear left to begin the loop trail.

The trail winds through alternating stands of pines and oaks. Discarded pine needles carpet sections of the trail, cushioning footsteps and accentuating the quiet of the area.

The trail leads sharply left as you begin to see Sengekontacket Pond, then turns right and leads to a pond overlook. Along the distant edge of this tidal pond, you'll see the Edgartown/Oak Bluffs Road. The pond attracts both migratory waterfowl and local islanders who drag its waters for scallops.

The path meanders away from the pond through an area with many clumps of reindeer lichen. This lichen grows in the soil in patches up to 10 inches in diameter. Its individual stalks resemble miniature deer antlers, and it is a basic food for reindeer in arctic areas.

After returning to the woods, the trail crosses a private road and switches back to parallel a salt marsh for awhile. Both snowy and common egrets may be within the marsh's confines. These birds frequent salt marshes and estuaries along the Atlantic seaboard. The common egret is the larger of the two, with a length of 32 inches and wingspan of 55 inches. It has a yellow bill and glossy black feet and legs. The smaller snowy egret grows to 20 inches long and has a wingspan of 38 inches. Its bill and legs are black, but its feet are yellow.

Distance (round trip): 1.1 miles

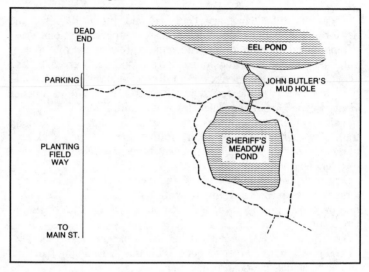

From Vineyard Haven, follow the signs for West Tisbury, Chilmark, and Gay Head for .4 miles. Turn left at the sign for Edgartown and drive 6 miles to the sanctuary sign on the left. Park along the roadside.

Leading into woods again, the path crosses back over the private road, heads through oaks, and passes a solitary white pine. As the path connects with the original fork, bear left and return to your car.

28. Sheriff's Meadow Wildlife Preserve

In 1956, from his home overlooking Sheriff's Meadow Pond, Henry Beetle Hough noticed that an ice house had been torn down. Learning that the land around the pond was to be opened up for development, he bought the first parcel of what was to become the Sheriff's Meadow Wildlife Preserve with the $500 he had recently received for writing his first book. Borrowing additional money, Henry succeeded in buying all the parcels around Sheriff's Meadow Pond, but he couldn't afford to pay the taxes on them. He tried unsuccessfully to interest foundations in the properties and eventually created the Sheriff's Meadow Foundation himself. Over the years, more tracts of land have been given to the Foundation and new trails have been established. Donations may be sent to: Sheriff's Meadow Foundation, Edgartown, MA 02539.

The sanctuaries of the Sheriff's Meadow Foundation offer chances to escape from crowds and congestion, renew one's senses in natural settings, walk undisturbed, discover Martha's Vineyard's varied character, and see wildlife in natural habitats. Voluntary contributions support the foundation's efforts to preserve, administer, and maintain natural wildlife habitats for education and conservation. Hunting, trapping, camping, and picnicking are prohibited.

The narrow footpath weaves through pines and spruces before leading into a meadow filled with ox-eye daisies and young trees. As you reach a trail junction and turn left, you have left any reminders of civilization behind.

After winding through heavy side growth, the path suddenly opens out onto a watery setting. To the left is John Butler's Mud Hole with Eel Pond and Vineyard Sound beyond. To the right is Sheriff's Meadow Pond, an old ice pond that now provides a haven for varied animal life.

Approach the wooden footbridge ahead quietly and look across Eel Pond for signs of waterfowl. One of the more interesting birds to spot is the common loon. Note the low silhouette, large, dark head, and (in summer) cross-banded back. Although silent in winter, the loon's yodel-like laugh can be heard frequently during the rest of the year, especially at night. Powerful feet attached at the rear of the body give extra leverage in water but make for awkward movements on land. Loons come ashore only to breed and nest.

Distance (around pond): .6 miles

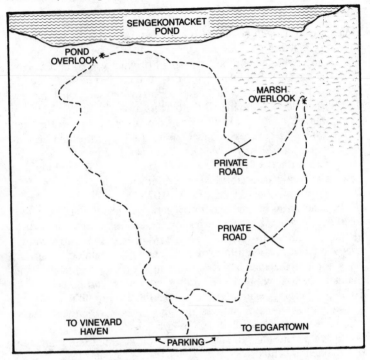

To reach the preserve in Edgartown (only one of the foundation's many sanctuaries on Martha's Vineyard), follow signs from Vineyard Haven to Edgartown. Turn left at the monument on Main Street onto Pease's Point Way. As this road bends sharply right a short distance ahead, continue straight onto Planting Field Way. Proceed down Planting Field Way for .2 miles to the Shurtleff Pumping Station and park along the side of the road. The trail begins directly across the street at the small sign.

Cross the footbridge and swing right through a tunnel of trees. A clearing ahead momentarily breaks the closeness of overhead branches and provides another view of Eel Pond. Continue along the path as it tunnels through trees and shrubs. In this darkened setting use your ears to detect animal activity and your sense of smell to recognize flowering shrubs.

At another clearing ahead you can rest upon a bench while surveying your surroundings. Listen for the red-winged blackbird's liquid *konk-ka-ree* call. The red, yellow-bordered shoulder patch identifies the otherwise black male. Females resemble large sparrows with heavier streaking and longer bills. The promiscuous males may mate with several females in each breeding season.

Continuing past the pond's far corner, the trail swings sharply right. Pitch pine needles soften the footing as you reach another clearing with views across the pond. The path winds through cedars and spruces back to the initial trail junction. Turn left for the short walk back to your starting point.

About the Authors

Whenever the Sadliers can escape from indoors, they are out of doors—hiking, walking, jogging, canoeing, camping. Their enthusiasm for nature is captivating.

Heather attended Vassar College and received a B.A. in Psychology and an M.Ed. in Education from the University of New Hampshire. Hugh received a B.A. in Sociology from Bates College and an M.Ed. in Recreation from Springfield College. They have written three other books on hiking in Maine, Vermont, and Massachusetts. The Sadliers live on the Maine coast.